The Post

ALICE PAUL FORMS NATIONAL WOMAN'S PARTY: 1916

The News

SUFFRAGE AMENDMENT RATIFIED BY 36TH STATE! WOMEN WIN RIGHT TO VOTE! 1920

THE CHRONICLE

WAR BREAKS OUT IN EUROPE! 1914

The Post

TED STATES NTERS WAR! 1917

The News

WOMEN ACROSS AMERICA VOTE IN ELECTION! 1920

THE CHRONICLE

ORLD WAR ENDS IN EUROPE! 1918

The Sun

ALICE PAUL LEADS STATE-BY-STATE CAMPAIGN TO RATIFY SUFFRAGE AMENDMENT: 1919

LECTED

For Radine, women's-rights champion and mom —D.R.

To my dear family, who always lift me up higher —N.Z.

THIS IS A BORZOI BOOK PUBLISHED BY ALFRED A. KNOPF

Text copyright © 2016 by Dean Robbins

Jacket art and interior illustrations copyright © 2016 by Nancy Zhang

Hand-lettering copyright © 2016 by Jeanine Henderson Murch

All rights reserved. Published in the United States by Alfred A. Knopf,

an imprint of Random House Children's Books, a division of Penguin Random House LLC, New York.

Knopf, Borzoi Books, and the colophon are registered trademarks of Penguin Random House LLC.

Visit us on the Web! randomhousekids.com

Educators and librarians, for a variety of teaching tools, visit us at RHTeachersLibrarians.com

Library of Congress Cataloging-in-Publication Data

Names: Robbins, Dean, author.

Title: Miss Paul and the president : the creative campaign for women's right

to vote / Dean Robbins ; illustrated by Nancy Zhang.

Description: New York : Knopf Books for Young Readers, 2016.

Summary: "The story of suffragette Alice Paul and her campaign to win women the right to vote." –Provided by publisher

Identifiers: LCCN 2015051182 (print) | LCCN 2016007268 (ebook) | ISBN 978-1-101-93720-4 (trade) |

ISBN 978-1-101-93721-1 (lib. bdg.) | ISBN 978-1-101-93722-8 (ebook)

Subjects: LCSH: Paul, Alice, 1885–1977–Juvenile literature. | Suffragists–United States–Biography–Juvenile literature. |

Women–Suffrage–United States–History–Juvenile literature. | Women's rights–United States–History–Juvenile literature. |

BISAC: JUVENILE NONFICTION / Biography & Autobiography / Women. | JUVENILE NONFICTION /

Girls & Women. | JUVENILE NONFICTION / History / United States / General.

Classification: LCC JK1899.P38 R64 2016 (print) | LCC JK1899.P38 (ebook) |

DDC 324.6/23092–dc23

LC record available at http://lccn.loc.gov/2015051182

The illustrations in this book were created using watercolor, colored pencil, and other media.

MANUFACTURED IN CHINA

September 2016

10 9 8 7 6 5 4 3 2 1

First Edition

MISS PAUL and the PRESIDENT

THE CREATIVE CAMPAIGN FOR WOMEN'S RIGHT TO VOTE

by **DEAN ROBBINS**

illustrated by **NANCY ZHANG**

Alfred A. Knopf · New York

ALICE PAUL hurried up and down
Pennsylvania Avenue in a purple hat.
She wanted to make everything perfect for her parade.
A parade no one in Washington, D.C., would ever forget!

Alice double-checked the twenty-six floats.
And the ten bands.
And the dozens of dancers.

She took her place with eight thousand other women.
They wore colorful sashes and carried brightly painted signs.

LET WOMEN VOTE IN THE 1914 ELECTION!

OUR SUPPORT!

WOMEN ARE CITIZENS, TOO!

LET WOMEN VOTE IN THE 1914 ELECTION!

Alice held on to her hat so it wouldn't blow off in the wind.
She led the women up Pennsylvania Avenue to the White House.
People lined the sidewalks to see the hullabaloo.
Some of them cheered.
But many jeered.
"NO to votes for women!" they called.

Alice expected the jeers.
Women couldn't vote in the United States,
and most Americans didn't think they should.
She hoped her parade would help to change their minds.

A mile away, Woodrow Wilson rode a train into Washington, D.C.
The new president of the United States adjusted his spectacles.
His daughter Margaret straightened his top hat.
"Thousands of people will be here to meet you," she said.
"You should look your best!"

THE CHRONICLE

CROWD TURNS OUT
FOR ALICE PAUL'S PARADE,
IGNORES NEW PRESIDENT!

President Wilson stepped off the train and waved.

But no one waved back.
The station was almost empty.
The whole city had gone to see
Alice Paul's parade instead!

Who *was* the determined young woman in the purple hat?

Alice Paul grew up on a farm.
She liked to make mischief right alongside the boys in her town.

They snuck candy.

And chased chickens.

And threw mud balls.

Every two years, Alice watched her father
go off to vote.
Her mother had to stay at home.
Why should it be that way?

Alice read about her country's laws.
The Constitution promised that people
could elect their own leaders.
But it also said that only men could vote.

Weren't women people, too?
Shouldn't they be able to vote as citizens
of the United States of America?

Alice found books on women's suffrage.
She learned that *suffrage* meant "the right to vote."
Suffragists wanted to change the Constitution so women
could help elect their own leaders, just as men did.
They needed to convince the president and Congress,
but the politicians in Washington, D.C., wouldn't listen.

Oh, Alice had lots of ideas for making them listen!
When she was old enough, she joined the other suffragists
who demanded the right to vote.
She impressed these women with her big parade
on Pennsylvania Avenue.
She impressed them even more when she set up a meeting
with President Woodrow Wilson himself.

President Wilson wanted to see the woman
who had caused the hullabaloo.
He thought she might apologize to him.
After all, she had stolen the spotlight on his first day
in Washington, D.C.

Alice did NOT plan to apologize!
She sat down in the president's office
and looked him right in the eye.
"Mr. President, will you support the
vote for women?" she asked.

The president did not expect so bold a question
from this small woman in a purple hat.
"Miss Paul, the time is not right.
I have many more important problems
to worry about!"

President Wilson got to work on his problems.
Alice got to work, too.
She opened an office in Washington, D.C.,
for a new group called the National Woman's Party.
Thousands of women joined.
They called Alice their "dear little leader."

The dear little leader wanted to show the president
that women's rights were as important as anything else
in the United States.

She would do it by making mischief, just as she had on the farm!

Margaret Wilson stared out the White House window.

"Father, come look!"

Alice led a fleet of fancy cars up Pennsylvania Avenue.

Women honked their horns and waved their yellow flags.

Congressmen came out of the Capitol to find a long scroll unfurled on the marble steps.

SUPPORT THE VOTE FOR WOMEN!

A funny-looking train chugged
from the East Coast to the West Coast.
Alice had named it the Suffrage Special.
The train stopped in towns along the way,
and families came out to gawk at it.
Women made speeches from the caboose.
"Send a letter to the president! Tell him to
support women's right to vote!"

President Wilson got bags of letters
from all around the country.
They piled up to the ceiling in his office.
But the president had other problems to worry about.
He didn't take time to read the letters about women's suffrage.

So Margaret read them instead.

That winter, Margaret sat next to
her father in the president's car.
A strange sight greeted them
at the White House gate.
Women strode back and forth carrying signs.

President Wilson spotted Alice at the
front of the group.
She looked him right in the eye.
The president glanced down at his newspaper,
but Margaret waved at Alice through the window.

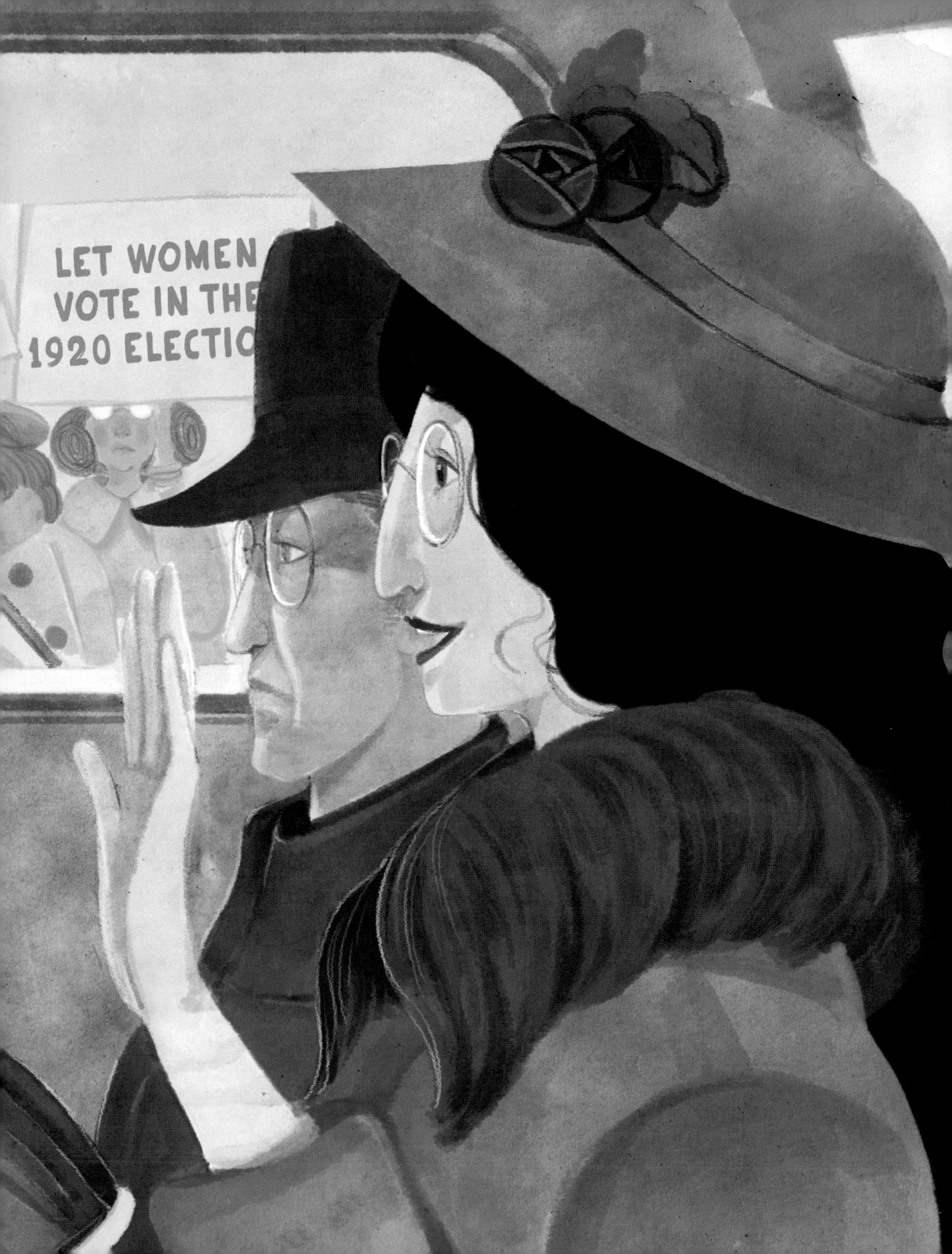
LET WOMEN
VOTE IN THE
1920 ELECTIO

Alice and her friends paced in front of the White House
day after day in the freezing cold.
People lined the sidewalks to see the hullabaloo.
Some of them jeered.
But many cheered.
They brought scarves and mittens to keep the women warm.

★ ★ ★ The Post ★
ALICE PAUL GETS OUT OF JAIL!
SAYS WOMEN PLAN TO KEEP GETTING
ARRESTED UNTIL PRESIDENT LISTENS

The police ordered Alice to leave the White House grounds.
"Not until the president supports women's right to vote!"
she declared.

The police put the women in handcuffs and took them off to jail.
Just as Alice hoped they would!

President Wilson did not like the thought of Alice in jail.
He knew she loved the United States.
Why else would she go to all this trouble to vote
in her country's elections?
"Maybe women's suffrage is more important
than I thought," he said.

Margaret looked her father right in the eye.
Just the way Alice Paul had.
"Yes to the vote for women!" she said.

The president would make a speech.
An important speech.

Alice stood with others from the National Woman's Party.
She wondered what the president would say.

Woodrow Wilson adjusted his spectacles.
Margaret straightened his tie.
"People all over the country will read about your speech,"
she said. "You should look your best!"

The president faced the crowd.
"The time is right! I will ask Congress to pass a law
giving all women the vote!"

The women waved yellow handkerchiefs
and threw yellow flowers.
"Three cheers for President Wilson!" they shouted.
"And three cheers for Alice Paul!"

Two years later, Alice skipped down Pennsylvania Avenue
to vote in the 1920 election.
She filled out her ballot and raised her arm in victory.

AUTHOR'S NOTE

Alice Paul and the National Woman's Party had a lot of work to do after convincing President Woodrow Wilson to support women's right to vote in 1918. They still needed Congress to change the Constitution. The women held meetings with many congressmen, and the president helped by making speeches in favor of women's suffrage.

After many twists and turns, Congress passed the Nineteenth Amendment to the Constitution on June 4, 1919. But the battle wasn't over! Thirty-six state governments had to approve the amendment before it could become law. Alice threw herself into the campaign by giving talks, sending hundreds of letters around the country, and speaking with every politician who might help. She also asked supporters to march through the streets dressed in yellow, the favorite color of the women's suffrage movement.

One by one, thirty-five state governments voted in favor of the amendment. It all came down to Tennessee, where the vote was tied. The youngest politician in the state, Harry Burn, had not yet voted, unsure of what to do. Then he got a letter from his mother that said, "Hurrah and vote for suffrage!" Harry did, and the Nineteenth Amendment finally became a part of the Constitution on August 26, 1920.

Millions of American women voted for the first time in the 1920 election, including a very happy Alice Paul.

BIBLIOGRAPHY

Adams, Katherine H., and Michael L. Keene. *Alice Paul and the American Suffrage Campaign.*
    Champaign, IL: University of Illinois Press, 2007.

Baker, Jean H. *Sisters: The Lives of America's Suffragists.* New York: Hill and Wang, 2006.

Cahill, Bernadette. *Alice Paul, the National Woman's Party and the Vote: The First Civil Rights Struggle of the 20th Century.* Jefferson, NC: McFarland, 2015.

Lunardini, Christine. *Alice Paul: Equality for Women* (Lives of American Women).
    Boulder, CO: Westview Press, 2012.

Walton, Mary. *A Woman's Crusade: Alice Paul and the Battle for the Ballot.*
    London: Palgrave Macmillan, 2010.

Zahniser, J. D., and Amelia R. Fry. *Alice Paul: Claiming Power.*
    New York: Oxford University Press, 2014.

The News
JAILED WOMEN PICKETERS GO ON HUNGER STRIKE! 1917

The Post
PRESIDENT WILSON ISSUES STATEMENT SUPPORTING WOMEN'S SUFFRAGE: 1918

THE CHRONICLE
UNITED STATES CONGRESS PASSES SUFFRAGE AMENDMENT: 1919

THE CHRONICLE
PRESIDENT WILSON ADDRESSES U.S. SENATE IN SUPPORT OF SUFFRAGE AMENDMENT: 1918

The News
SUFFRAGE LEADER ALICE PAUL CASTS HER FIRST BALLOT! 1920

The Post
WOODROW WILSON ELECTED TO SECOND TERM AS PRESIDENT! 1916

The Sun
INDIVIDUAL STATES GRANT LIMITED VOTING RIGHTS, BUT SUFFRAGISTS SEEK CONSTITUTIONAL AMENDMENT: 1914